Words Covered In Salt

Table of Contents

<u>February</u>

It's a February night

You're calling me instead of her

Hitting me up for a late night kiss

Where's your girlfriend on nights like this

Unexpected Fire

He's an asshole

An asshole that you will easily come to adore

from the moment he walks up to you

He'll take his sunglasses off

and his piercing hazel eyes will light a fire in you

that you thought you didn't have anymore

3 Months

It's been 3 months

3 months since I've seen you in person

3 months since I walked out that apartment door

Tears streaming down my face

and yours blank

3 months since I couldn't muster up the words to

say goodbye

3 months since I drove away from that small

Wisconsin town

Tears streaming down my face

3 months that I've tried not to talk to you

and 3 times that I've failed

<u>My Final Goodbye</u>

Why don't you understand that you could have

everything going for you if you tried

You're so smart

The kind of smart that people hide away and they

shouldn't

But you're also the kind of guy who makes wrong

choices over and over again

You know they aren't right and you continue to

make them

I feel for you in some way, I do

I want to help you, but you can't be helped

There comes a point when a girl has to give up

I'm giving up quickly, I know I am, but I've been

through too much to try and make this work

This will hurt me more later on if I don't let you go

now

I can't watch you destroy your life and be okay with

it

So this is my final goodbye

Thinking Of You

It's 2 am

I'm thinking of you

I wish there was more to say

but your heads somewhere else

And mines stuck on you

"What If I Said This?"

Just do it. Tell the person you want to tell.

Whatever you've been dying to tell them or ask

them, do it.

In all reality you probably don't have time to be

constantly stressing about whether you should let

someone know something or not.

Get it out of the way.

What's the worst that can happen?

So what if they tell you they don't feel the same

way, or they just want to be friends.

Move on, find someone new and maybe they'll

have the answer you're looking for.

I don't have the time to wait around for someone

and neither should you.

Gold & Garbage

I'm gold

And you're nothing

but garbage on the floor

Moments

I can't explain what you mean to me

or where I'd be without you in my life

There's a part of me that sits around waiting for you

like an abandoned dog waiting for their owner to

come home

but they never show

You very well might be the reason I can't find

someone that means anything to me

No one is you

No one can look at me the way you do and make me

feel like everything's going to be okay

For that moment it will be okay

I'll be with you and time will stand still

I'll forget about the fact that I have to go home

without you and that you don't feel the way I do

I live for those okay moments

To The Person Who Broke Me

Thank you to the person who broke me

Because you broke me I'm the person I am today

Thank you for making me feel like I was never

enough

Feeling this way made me strive to be better than

the person I thought I was

I learned that I can't be better and to accept myself

for whom I really am

I tried so hard to be the right person for you

but I somehow never was despite how much you

tried to convince me otherwise

Thank you for showing me that it was you who

wasn't good enough for me

It's Only A Façade

She smiles everyday even though deep inside she's

drowning

She wears her smile so proudly that no one notices

it's a façade.

STOP

Stop. Stop whatever the fuck you're doing right now. I'm talking to you. The one who's in love with someone she can't ever have; someone who will never love you back. You're fucking killing yourself. Everyday you're killing yourself. Yeah, you may go through your day and if you don't see him you're fine, but at night what happens? I don't even have to tell you. You fucking know what happens. You lay there and think about the what ifs and the possibilities. Well there are none honey. That's life. He doesn't love you back. That's the pain of it all. And what happens when you see him tomorrow? You're friends, yeah that's cool. Hang out, talk and laugh like everything's fine. It's not. You know it, your friends know it, hell even he knows it, but he doesn't do anything about it. And you don't deserve that. Loving someone who doesn't love you is killing you. It's holding you

back from the possibility of finding someone who

will actually love you. It hurts. I know it does. It

fucking hurts seeing him and acting like everything

is cool. It's not fucking cool. Kill it before it kills

you.

Your Mom

Didn't your mother ever tell you to not fuck over

someone you claimed to love?

A Risk I Can't Take

I'm constantly longing for something that I can't

reach

Adventure, danger, you

Things that linger in the distance, close enough for

me to see, but too risky to touch

Things that could shatter me, or things that could

make me whole again

Wish It Were You

You're going to see her with someone else one day

and you're going to wish it were you

You're going to wish you didn't leave her when you

did for all those stupid reasons you had weighing in

the back of your mind

She'll be bright, beautiful, and bubblier than ever

And you'll never have her back

Faded Memories

The stories that you post bring up memories that

can't be forgotten

So embedded in my head that the vivid images

never blur

Faded memories and times that maybe had no

meaning to you

Are forever stuck with me

Nothing

I don't let myself like anyone anymore

I've been hurt too many times to try

Every road, every new day, every new person

Leads down the exact same path

Heartache, sadness, emptiness

Why choose me, and then leave

Leave like it's nothing

Like I was nothing

Maybe I am nothing

Mistakes

There are times when I want to erase everything

I've ever known about you

Wipe away those months we spent together

Maybe I loved you, but you didn't have an impact

on my life other than the toll you're taking now

Just someone who was there and left without

warning

Deleted

Maybe you didn't want to take pictures because you

didn't want to have to go back and erase what

couldn't be undone.

Memories deleted from your phone, but forever in

your head.

Wasted Time

I put all of my emotions and energy into people who

couldn't care less about me when I should be

investing that time into people who do

What I Deserve

You were my first love

Loving you was the hardest thing I've ever done

It was exhausting and it was something I never truly

got in return

Since I loved you it taught me that someone one day

Will have enough heart to love me the way I

deserve

My Person

Doesn't everyone have that person?

The one you hear their name,

And each time you die a little more inside.

Stay Awake

Lying awake at night

I can almost feel your touch linger

The nights we stayed awake far too long

are nothing but a memory

Times I can never get back

But only hope they'll come again

<u>Reality</u>

I only think about you late at night when my mind

won't stop

Swirling around the idea that I'll see you again

It's not reality

but reality was never something I was fond of

anyway

Travesty

Because of you I'm distant with everyone I meet

Scared to be touched

I flinch away from the thought of someone truly

caring about me

And their fingers tracing the outline of my body

with a gentle touch

Never kind, helpful, or loving

Only a false representation of yourself

A true travesty

<u>Wishful Thinking</u>

My eyes are tired and my mind won't stop

Images imprinted in the beds of my eyelids

Hoping to get some peace, but knowing that's

wishful thinking

Listen

Listen you beautiful motherfucker

He doesn't deserve you

You're a badass bitch that doesn't need someone

who is only going to use you

Don't let him trick you into thinking you're

someone special because you're probably just

another girl on his fuck list

And you don't deserve that

Be the beautiful woman you are and find a man who

loves you

Dying Light

It's four in the morning and we're sitting together

Talking about anything and everything

Rolling on and on

You're opening up about times you've never shared

with anyone

A glimmer of hope sprinkles light inside me

that you'll continue to let me in

Another week goes by and its 4 am again

Laying together in the dark you whisper

through drunken words about how much you care

Yet another glimmer of hope

One more week and you're gone

And the light slowly dies

Miss Me

You'll start off as friends

but a friend that you can't get enough of

You'll find ways to hangout everyday

Staying out later than you probably should

Going for three hour long walks

Talking endlessly will have never felt so easy

And you'll miss him when he's gone

and you'll wish he missed you too

Cheated

You cheated on me countless times

You thought you hurt me more than yourself

but I'm learning otherwise

You lost someone who loved you despite

everything you did

Someone who could love your every flaw

And for that

You are the one hurting more than me

Broken

Thank you for tearing me down to nothing

both physically and emotionally.

You left me with nothing but bruises, anxiety, and

broken promises.

I now know what love doesn't feel like.

I know what shouldn't happen in a relationship and

how someone who loves me shouldn't treat me.

You were right all along. You didn't deserve me,

but because of you I'm stronger than I ever was

before.

I don't let people put me down.

I know how to stand up for myself.

I'm able to get up everyday and move on despite the

insecurities you put into my head.

I have the ability to smile and laugh through the

pain you put me through.

If it weren't for you I wouldn't have gone through

all that hurt. I wouldn't be afraid to be alone for a

long period of time because being alone gives me

time to think about how much you broke me

But without you

I wouldn't be the person I am today.

Warning

I'll never know why I think about you all the time

Maybe because you entered my life so suddenly

And at a time when I needed you the most

Left me without warning

Sudden and quick

Still at a time when I needed you

Secrets

I want to take everything back

The secrets I shared were never meant for someone

like you to hear

Silly me for assuming that you could be someone I

could trust

I never thought you would leave and take my

secrets with

Turned Away

Months have passed and you're still tearing me

apart

Hitting me up at random times

You were never there when I needed you

So there's no need to reach out now

I stop myself from responding

Knowing I'm bettering myself each time I turn you

away

I'm Sorry I'm Not Sorry

I'm sorry felt like the only words I used to say

You would hurt me unconditionally and twist my

mind into thinking I was in the wrong

So I would apologize

It's been three years since we've last seen each

other

And I still do this

Every time I say those two words I think of you

You're the last person I want on my mind

And for that

I'm not sorry

I Hope You're Missing Me Like I'm Missing You

Mind wandering late at night about the times shared

and the memories made

I try and snap myself out of my nightly routine of

reminiscing about the past

Wondering if you ever think about the same things I

do

Only fooling myself

I close my eyes and try to stop missing you

Forgiven

Forgive yourself for the times you can't get back

And the times you spent with people who never

cared about you in the first place

<u>Untitled</u>

The drunken words you spoke are forever stuck in

my sober mind

Made, Lost, Wasted

Are you happy

With the choices you've made

The people you've lost

And the hours you've wasted

Numb

I'm numb from feeling anything anymore

No happiness, sadness, or anger

An entire body once filled with love

Is only left with emptiness

Stitches

I've ruined myself over and over for you

And you never once tried to put me back together

Falling apart I had to stitch myself up time and time

again

Only to be ripped open further each time by

something called "love"

Drained And Tired

It's fucking tough going through everyday feeling

drained and tired

Not wanting to get out of bed

but not having a sufficient enough reason to stay put

So you roll out and continue living your drained and

tired life

Leave While You Can

You're being torn apart in every which way letting

this person control your life

You need to find a way out

Get out of there and don't look back

You either think you deserve this of they're

convincing you that you do

And you don't

No one deserves to be walked all over like a worn

out doormat

So if you're looking for a sign

This is it

Fucking leave

You won't regret it

Win Or Lose

What did I really end up losing anyway?

A boy who wouldn't appreciate me?

Someone who wouldn't get back to me when I

called?

What they lost is a girl who would care for them

and accept them for everything they were.

A girl who would never turn their back on them.

So who's really losing?

Goodbye Never

It's hard getting over someone you never had

All the made up scenarios in your head that never

played out as if you hoped they would

The words never exchanged

And the goodbye you never had

An Exquisite Waste Of Time

There are people who have came in and out of my

life that were a complete waste of time

But they played a role in shaping who I am as a

person

Without them I wouldn't be sitting here writing this

now

And for that they were an exquisite waste of time

Nothing But A Cheat

If he leaves you don't let him back in your life

Please don't do it

He'll come crawling back after he's fucked around

with other girls

Bringing back nothing but empty promises

Promises that will coo to your ear

Only making you let him back in

And then he'll do the same thing again

He'll leave

He'll cheat

And he'll come back

As if the last time he fucked up never happened

And you're supposed to welcome him back into

your life after he's torn it apart

He'll think you're supposed to accept his fake

apologies and think he'll never do it again

And you'll probably believe him

In the end you'll wish you hadn't

So if you have the chance

Get rid of him while you can

<u>Feels</u>

Catching feelings for someone is a roller coaster of

emotions that usually ends in death

Still Holding On

I hate that I'm still holding onto hope

That the day will come when you decide you want

me as more than a friend

That the one summer night we shared together was

something more than a drunken mistake

And that the way you look at me isn't something all

in my head

Drowning

I don't know what I hate drowning in more

My thoughts or silence

Pain

If only you could feel the pain she feels when your

name pops up

It's coming down to deleting you from her history

not only online but in her mind as well

Only to try and rid the pain that aches so deep

you could feel it on the other side of the world

Compliment

I don't accept compliments anymore because they

sound foreign

A made up lie to try and get close to me

Only to desert me in the end

A Cry For Help

Crying on the bathroom floor

She's been there too many times to count

Always reaching out to the same person for comfort

And he always comes when she needs him

He tells her to stay away from the guys she's talking

to and she knows she should listen

Maybe it's a cry for help

Or maybe it's a cry for you

Sad Song

Sad songs seem to be so much sadder

When you're living one

Don't Worry About Me

Don't worry about hurting me

Making me sad, angry, or disappointing me

Don't worry about letting me down

And don't feel bad when you leave

The broke can't be re-broken

The Old Me

I don't know if I miss the old me

The me before I unraveled

I don't know who I was back then

<u>Off</u>

There came a point when I stopped fighting because

I simply didn't care anymore

I didn't care if we were together

Broken up

Or if you were dying beside me

My emotions were turned off

And I didn't feel the slightest

Could Have Been

I can't keep investing in someone who is never

going to want me

I go through my day hoping you'll reach out to me

and the time never comes

Yet I continue the next in hope of the same thing

It's better to realize you're never coming after me

than to waste my life dreaming about you

And missing out on chances I should have taken

What Matters

It doesn't matter what you did in the beginning to

make me happy

It matters that in the end I was crying everyday

I was depressed and anxious

I was scared to leave because I didn't want you to

hurt me

And I didn't have the nerve to tell anyone what you

were doing to me

It matters that you broke me down in a way I will

never forget

And that I will forever be rebuilding myself

Badass

Why are you fighting for someone who doesn't

want you?

And especially doesn't deserve you?

Find someone who deserves the badass sassy bitch

you are.

If You Don't Want Me

I will not beg you to want me

I've learned my lesson

If you don't want me then so be it

I will not chase you

I will not ask why you aren't choosing me

In the end I know I'm not lo

sing out on anything

But you're going to find out you lost out on me

Losing Sleep

You're losing sleep over a boy who is sleeping

peacefully next to another girl

A boy who doesn't bat an eye when you walk by

while other boys are fawning over you

A boy who doesn't lose a wink of sleep because of

you

You're losing sleep over a boy who is nothing to

you

And everything to someone else

Ask Him

If he's hiding you from his friends and family

Not posting about you and only loving you behind a

curtain

Ask yourself why

Better yet ask him

Plan B

I am not a backup plan

When the girl that you left me for doesn't work out

(And I know it won't)

Don't come back to me

I don't want to hear from you

And I'm not going to pick up the broken pieces

because she broke your heart

I still have to pick up mine

The Hard Part

It's easy to tell myself I'm over you

But when I see you

To try and not love everything about you

The way you look at me

And the way you know how I'm feeling without

having to ask

Now that's the hard part

Almost

We were almost something

Not together

Not a part

But almost

It's Okay

It took a really long time for me to realize that guys

aren't everything

I can live a happy single life

I have my friends

I have my family

I have my animals

There isn't a need to add a constant stress to my life

A constant worry about who I'll talk to next

And why they don't feel the same way as I do

It's okay to be alone

Dying

I lost my mind trying to figure out how yours

worked

How you could treat someone you supposedly loved

with such hatred

And watch me slowly die inside

Without even batting an eye

<u>Trust</u>

One day I brought you home to meet my family and

the next you broke my heart

There's a reason I don't trust anyone anymore

To Hell And Back

I've learned so much about myself these past few

years

From how to love and how to be loved

To why I'm not the person I used to be

Time changes a lot

Especially a person who's been through hell and

back

<u>A Ten Word Story</u>

I loved you so much I lost myself

How stupid

A Chance

You once told me I "let people walk all over me"

And you didn't try and help me change myself for

the better

Instead you saw it as a chance to put on your shoes

and crush me

To Live Or Die

I don't think a person really knows pain until

they're crying so hard they can't breath anymore

Lying on the ground fighting for air

Fighting for a life they aren't sure they want to live

It's Too Late

I'm so used to being hurt that I don't realize when

people are doing it

I find excuses for what they're doing and let it go

on before it's too late

Think Twice

I fought for you like nothing else mattered in this

world

I was willing to drop everything

Do anything to get you back

When you didn't even think twice about leaving me

"You Never Loved Me"

I did love you

But I had to let you go

You were killing me in every way possible and I

couldn't breathe anymore

I couldn't fall asleep at night

And when I did

I didn't want to wake up

Secluding myself from everyone sounded better

than trying to put on a fake smile and hide the pain I

was going through

And when I did find the strength to go about my

day

You would find ways to try and drag me down and

make me feel guilty

So I would have to sit in the same room as you and

never leave

Never see anyone else

I would be yours forever

Isolating me from my friends and family

And that's why I had to leave

Because you didn't really love me

Home

I was scared

So scared of the hand coming at me

I'd crawl as far to the other side of the bed as I

could

But it still managed to reach me

Dragged from my own bed

I was forced to sleep on the floor

Scared of the place and the person

I called home

Together Or Alone

Love is an amazing thing

Keeping you up laughing together

Or crying yourself to sleep alone

Move On

Move on

Move on

Move on

Move on

Move on

It's done

It's over

Caught

A guy who hides their feelings is never going to

work out in a relationship

They're going to be too caught up with themselves

To be caught up in you

Self-Explanatory

Fuck him.

If he doesn't have the time to talk to you than don't

waste yours on him.

<u>Sinking</u>

It may feel like you're sinking now but the time will

come when you feel you're finally above water

swimming towards shore

<u>Suddenly</u>

And all of the sudden I felt okay

I saw you and didn't think twice about wanting you

back

The Voice

You'll text him one day despite the voice in the

back of your mind telling you not to

And he won't reply

And you'll find out the voice was right

I Shouldn't Have

I shouldn't have replied to your message

I shouldn't have met up with you

And fell so hopelessly in love

So goddamn fast

But I did

And I can't change what happened between us

I can only sit here and write about the times we

shared

And wish I never replied

Small

Get out of this small town while you can before

these small town boys kill your big time heart

Made in the USA
Middletown, DE
13 January 2020